THAILAND

THAILAND

BUDDHIST KINGDOM AT THE HEART OF SOUTHEAST ASIA

NARISA CHAKRABONGSE

amber
BOOKS

First published in a pocket flexibound edition in 2020

Copyright © 2022 Amber Books Ltd.

Published by Amber Books Ltd
United House
North Road
London N7 9DP
United Kingdom
www.amberbooks.co.uk
Instagram: amberbooksltd
Facebook: amberbooks
Twitter: @amberbooks
Pinterest: amberbooksltd

ISBN: 978-1-83886-234-3

Project Editor: Michael Spilling
Designer: Gary Webb
Picture Research: Terry Forshaw and Justin Willsdon

Printed in China

Contents

Introduction

At the heart of Southeast Asia, the kingdom of Thailand is full of contrasts. Its long history and successive kingdoms, as well as immigration from nearby countries – in particular China – over several centuries, has made the country ethnically and cultural diverse. Renowned for food, beaches, friendly people and a relaxed lifestyle, this guide shows just how much there is to explore. With 40,000 temples throughout the country and 97 per cent of the population being Theravada Buddhists, the religion pervades everyday life. In addition, respect for the monarchy, albeit a constitutional one since 1932, remains powerful.

Each region of Thailand is very different, from the mountainous north and northeast, to the historic sites of Sukhothai and Ayutthaya in the centre, and glorious beaches in the east, west and south. Thailand is a biodiversity hotspot and the national parks are a lesser-known delight. At the centre is Bangkok, one of the most vibrant cities in the world.

ABOVE:
Fishmonger, Yaowarat Road, Chinatown, Bangkok
A woman in traditional palm-leaf hat pedals her cart on a pedestrian crossing in Chinatown, one of the biggest Chinatown's in the world.

OPPOSITE:
Golden Buddha, Wat Phra That Khao Noi, Nan Province
The elegant nine-metre (30-ft) high walking Buddha image, dominating the skyline above Nan town, was installed in December 1999 to commemorate the birthday of the late King Bhumibhol, King Rama IX.

Bangkok

Bangkok, capital of Thailand and a so-called primate city of 15 million people, is full of contrasts, allowing one to time travel from peaceful tradition to ultra-modern in a heartbeat. Sleek skyscrapers house shopping malls full of the latest tech gadgets and high-end brands, while down narrow backstreets and quiet canals one can find glittering temples and traditional communities.

Known by the Thais as Krung Thep Maha Nakhon, in the 17th century the small riverine settlement of Bangkok controlled shipping and trade goods on their way up the Chao Phraya River to the former capital of Ayutthaya. After the fall of that city in 1767, Bangkok was officially founded in 1782 by King Rama I, the first king of the current Chakri dynasty.

Founded on the east bank of the Chao Phraya river, almost 250 years ago, the city has spread north and east to cover an area of 1568 sq kilometres (606 sq miles).

Infamous for traffic jams and nightlife, the capital is also home to 400 Buddhist temples, countless markets, including the world-renowned Chatuchak weekend market, mouth-watering street-food stalls, over 25 Michelin-starred restaurants and a growing art and cultural scene. Truly it is a city with something for everyone.

OPPOSITE:

The Grand Palace and Wat Pho

The Grand Palace is the heart of old Bangkok and former home to the first five kings of the Chakri dynasty. Today, it is still used for important royal ceremonies.

On the left is the Chakri Maha Prasat throne hall, while to the right is the nearby royal temple of Wat Pho, and in the background the tall towers of the modern city.

OVERLEAF:

Traffic on Silom Road

Bad traffic and tangled electricity cables are features of Bangkok streets. But Bangkok taxis are among the most colourful anywhere and are also cheap. Some drivers adorn the dashboards of their cabs with small shrines or tiny toys and, as many come from the Northeast, often play loud country music and have forthright political views.

RIGHT TOP:

Glutinous Rice Wrapped in Banana Leaf

Rice is a staple of the Thai diet. Many snacks mix sweet, sticky rice with nuts or fruit, wrapped in an eco-friendly banana leaf. Recently some supermarkets have reverted to wrapping fresh produce in banana leaves in a bid to reduce plastic packaging.

RIGHT BOTTOM:

Pad Thai Street Food Stall

This dish of rice noodles, bean curd, egg, dried shrimps and bean sprouts has become one of the world's favourite dishes. It is likely that the dish was originally introduced by the Chinese who immigrated to Thailand from Southern China, bringing their love of noodles with them.

OPPOSITE:

Talad Rot Fai Market

Browsing market stalls and bargaining gently with the stall owner is one of the great pleasures of living in, or visiting, Bangkok. Talad Rot Fai (literally 'train market'), opens Thursday to Sunday, specialises in vintage fashion and collectibles from the last century, including kitsch items and furniture, as well as having cool restaurants and food stalls.

Street Food

Thai cuisine is usually rated
in the top five of the world's
favourites, but interestingly
most Thais don't cook,
preferring to get takeaways
from such street stalls as
this, which proliferate all
over Bangkok and offer a
wide range of curries, stir-
fried vegetables and other
popular dishes.

Spirit-House Offerings

Spirit houses abound
throughout Thailand. Thais
were originally animists and,
believing that the 'spirit of
place' inhabits plots of land
and trees, continue to erect
small dwellings for the spirits
when building homes. Over
the years, offerings build up
at such shrines, especially at
those with a reputation for
granting wishes.

ALL PHOTOGRAPHS:

Yaowarat Road, Chinatown
The Chinese began immigrating to Thailand in the 19th century and quickly became important as traders and tax farmers. Today numbering over one million, most Chinese have intermarried and are totally integrated in Thai society. Chinatown, originally on the site of the Grand Palace was moved to its current position 250 years ago.

To the right, a chef cooks in a wok over an open flame on a street stall, while below locals eat in a typical outdoor restaurant in Chinatown.

Bhumibol Bridge (Industrial Ring Road Bridge)

Two seven-lane sections make up this spectacular bridge, with diamond-shaped pylons, crossing the Chao Phraya river twice where a large U-bend has a narrow neck. Inaugurated in 2006, it is named after King Bhumibol Adulyadej (King Rama IX), who died in 2017 and was one of the world's longest reigning monarchs. It forms part of a ring road linking Bangkok with Samut Prakan.

Erawan Shrine
Standing near the Erawan
Hyatt Hotel, this much-loved
shrine with an image of
the four-faced god Brahma
demonstrates the continued
presence of Brahmanism
in Thai spiritual life. Built
in 1956, the shrine soon
acquired the reputation of
granting wishes and devotees
repay successful outcomes
with marigold garlands
and traditional dance
performances.

LEFT:

Long-tail Boat

Long-tail boats, powered
by truck engines fitted with
propeller shafts, speed along
canals and the river, taking
commuters to work and
tourists on canal tours. In
the past, Thai settlements
developed ribbon-like along
canals. Trade was also
conducted on the water via
floating markets, leading
Bangkok at one time to be
known as the 'Venice of
the East'.

RIGHT:

**Chakrabongse Villas,
Ta Tien**

Once the home of Prince
Chakrabongse, a son of
King Chulalongkorn,
Chakrabongse Villas is today
a small boutique hotel.
Situated on the bank of the
Chao Phraya river almost
opposite Wat Arun, it has
unparalleled views and a
waterside restaurant serving
royal Thai cuisine.

RIGHT:

Chao Phraya River Boat
Rather than spending an hour in traffic, many choose to commute to work or meetings via river boat. Tourists also enjoy this way of jumping on and off to visit the historic sites along the river.

OPPOSITE:

Maeklong Railway Market, Samut Prakan
The Maeklong railway market, established in 1905, sells ordinary fresh fruit, vegetables and fish in an extraordinary way. The market stalls edge the tracks, with vendors simply retracting their umbrellas as a train approaches. Although it seems as if much of the produce will be crushed, once the train passes, selling calmly resumes.

OPPOSITE:

Emerald Buddha Temple Compound, the Grand Palace

Until the 20th century, the Grand Palace was the spiritual and administrative centre of the kingdom. Twelve three-metre (10-ft) tall giants guard the entrance gates to the compound.

Behind the giant is a golden *kinnaree*, one of the mythological creatures, half-human half-bird, believed to inhabit the Himaphan Forest around Mount Meru, home of the gods.

LEFT:

Demon Statues Guard a Gold Chedi, Emerald Buddha Temple Compound

The golden *chedi* (stupa) is one of a pair created by King Rama I (1782–1809) in honour of his father and his mother. Mosaic-covered monkeys and demons from the *Ramakien*, Thailand's version of the *Ramayana* epic, stand guard, the demons identifiable by their small tusks.

**Four Regnal Stupas,
Wat Pho**

Wat Pho, built by King Rama
I on the site of an earlier
temple, is the most important
of the royal Bangkok temples
and has been renovated
continuously over 250 years,
in particular by King Rama
III (r.1824–51). The 42-metre
(138-ft) high stupas are
dedicated to the first four
reigns of the Chakri dynasty.
The temple compound has
many stone Chinese statues,
two of which are seen here.

**The Reclining Buddha,
Wat Pho**

The 46-metre (150-ft)
reclining Buddha represents
the passage of the Buddha
into Nirvana and the end of
his cycle of death and rebirth.
It was built, together with the
surrounding *vihara*, in 1832.
The soles of the Buddha's
feet are divided into 108
panels depicting the
auspicious signs associated
with the Buddha in mother-
of-pearl on black lacquer.

**Dharmachakra on the
Soles of the Buddha's Feet,
Wat Pho**

The roundel at the centre
of each foot represents the
dharmachakra, or wheel
of the law. Mother-of-pearl
inlaid in black lacquer is an
intricate Thai craft which
can withstand both the hot,
humid climate and termites.
In the past, a department
of the "Ten Royal Crafts"
specialised in its creation.

OPPOSITE:

**Face of the Reclining
Buddha, Wat Pho**

In contrast with the densely
patterned columns, the
Buddha's face is serene. In
general, Thai art abhors
a vacuum and every
surface is usually adorned
with paintings or carved
decoration. Gold glimmers
everywhere, apart from the
Buddha image such as on the
ceiling and the cushion inlaid
with glass mosaic behind the
Buddha's head.

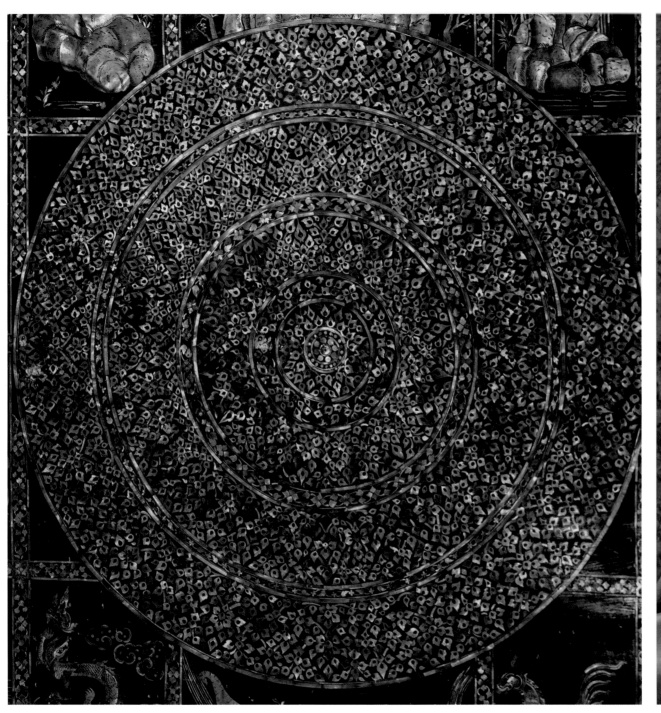

Jim Thompson's House, Rama I Road

Situated down a quiet *soi* (small lane) off busy Rama I road, the house is a treasure trove of Thai artefacts within the setting of several traditional Thai wooden houses, collected by Jim Thompson, founder in 1948 of the famous Thai Silk Company.

Thai vernacular architecture works using a modular system of panels which can be moved and re-erected with ease. Jim Thompson came to Thailand as part of the American Office for Strategic Service (OSS, a precursor to the CIA) towards the end of World War II, and never left. He disappeared in mysterious circumstances in 1967 while walking in the Cameron Highlands, Malaysia.

PREVIOUS PAGES LEFT:
Khao San Road
Khao San Road, near the river and major sites, is a long-time mecca for backpackers, offering simple rooms for a few hundred baht, cheap food stalls and fashion, as well as fake ID cards, driving licences and degrees. At nighttime the street truly comes alive, thronged with tourists shopping, eating and drinking in the bars which stay open till late.

PREVIOUS PAGES RIGHT:
Jek Pui Curry Stall, Yaowarat
This famous *khao gaeng* (curry and rice) street-food stall was established by the present owner's father over 50 years ago and is both cheap and very tasty. Customers sit on one of the red plastic chairs (red being an auspicious colour for Chinese) and wait for one of the waiters or waitresses to take their order.

RIGHT:
Tuk-tuks, Khao San Road
The three-wheeled tuk-tuk, a post-World War II development of the human-peddled rickshaw, has become an iconic symbol of Bangkok. Although often found in tourist hotspots such as Khao San Road, they are also used by locals, especially for awkward loads. Warnings about their safety abound in guidebooks and haggling the ride price is essential.

**Buddhaisawan Chapel,
National Museum**
Until the middle King
Chulalongkorn's reign
(reigned 1868–1910),
Thailand had a second
king, whose abode, known
as the 'Palace of the Front',
was almost as lavish as the
Grand Palace. Since 1924, the
Buddhaisawn Chapel (built
in 1795), housing the revered
15th century Phra Buddha
Sihing (lit. Sri Lankan) image,
has been part of the National
Museum. The murals along
the side walls show *devas*
in an attitude of prayer and
the carved wooden ceiling
is typical of the Bangkok
period.

RIGHT:
**Interior, Buddhaisawan
Chapel**
Maha Uparaj (Deputy
king) Maha Sura Singhanat
(1744–1804) had the chapel
decorated with murals, with
the back wall recounting the
Life of the Buddha. Here a
detail of that mural shows the
installation and worship of
the relics of the Buddha.

Sathorn Unique Tower
This 47-storey tower,
designed by Rangsan
Torsuwan, was begun in 1990
but fell victim first to the
architect becoming embroiled
in a murder plot (he was later
acquitted) and then to the
Asian financial crash of 1997.
It has since become an urban
exploration destination,
albeit an illegal one, with
various myths developed
around the 'ghost tower'.

Vertigo, Banyan Tree Hotel
Rooftop restaurants and
bars have become ever more
popular in Bangkok. Night-
time city views are impressive,
there is usually a cool breeze
and mosquitoes can't seem
to fly that high. One of
the earliest and a perennial
favourite is Vertigo, which has
both a small restaurant and
a bar on the 61st floor of the
Banyan Tree Hotel.

Bangkok Mass Transit System

With icy air conditioning, this elevated railway – popularly called the Skytrain – was formally opened on 5 December 1999. Over the past 20 years, various extensions have been added and certain stations connected with the MRT (Metropolitan Rapid Transit), or underground, finally pushing Bangkok towards a more integrated mass transit system.

LEFT:

Nang Kwak, **Museum Siam**
Towering over the room housing her is the four-metre (13-ft) high figure of *Nang Kwak* (literally 'beckoning lady'), believed by shopkeepers to bring good luck and encourage customers. She is part of a 14-room exhibition entitled 'Decoding Thainess', opened in 2017, which seeks to get behind the popular clichés of what it means to be Thai.

RIGHT:

Wat Benchamabophit, Dusit District
Often referred to as the Marble temple, this elegant building was designed by one of King Chulalongkorn's half-brothers, Prince Naris, in 1899, following the king's move to recently laid-out Dusit Park. The Italian marble temple, with its orange-tiled roofs, gilded barge boards and finials, *chofa*, is a wonderful example of classical Thai temple architecture.

LEFT:

Songkran

Among Thailand's various annual festivals, one of the most popular for locals and visitors alike is Songkran. In the past, the festival, celebrating Thai New Year over several days from 11–13th April, was centred on the temple and was an opportunity for young people to flirt. Today, it has become an excuse for raucous, fun-filled water fights.

ABOVE:

Thai Boxing, Ratchadamnoen Stadium

Thais excel internationally at traditional boxing, but in the last 30 years Muay Thai has also gained worldwide attention. Known as 'The Art of Eight Limbs', it allows the use of elbows, knees and shins. Developed from hand-to-hand combat during Thailand's many wars with her neighbours, it was in 1921 that the first ring opened for Muay Thai as a spectator sport.

RIGHT:
Seafood Feast
A serious Thai meal requires many dishes accompanied by rice. In the centre of this seafood array is *nam phrik*, a Thai dipping sauce made with fermented shrimp paste, eaten with fried Thai mackerel.

OPPOSITE TOP LEFT:
Freshly-carved Fruit
Vegetable carving has been elevated to an art form in Thailand. Here various melons are intricately carved, including one with the initials of HM Queen Sirikit the Queen Mother.

OPPOSITE TOP RIGHT:
Tom Yum Goong
Spicy prawn soup is one of Thai cuisine's most popular dishes. Not only delicious, its ingredients of galangal, lemon grass, kaffir lime leaves, fresh chilli and lime are said to have many health-giving properties.

OPPOSITE BOTTOM LEFT:
Stir-frying Pad Thai
Pad Thai looks simple, but the rice noodles must be soaked first and the ingredients call for tofu, bean sprouts, *kuaei chai* (garlic chives), dried shrimp, egg, tamarind and fish sauce.

OPPOSITE BOTTOM RIGHT:
Pork Satay
Originally from Java, satay dipped in peanut sauce and cucumber and chilli in vinegar has become extremely popular in Thailand, as it is easy to eat and not too spicy.

LEFT:

Buddhist Monk Collecting Alms

Getting up early to give alms to Buddhist monks is a long-standing Thai tradition, both in the cities and the countryside. Known as *tak bat* ('spooning food into the alms bowl'), in the past freshly-steamed rice would be served into the bowl together with a few dishes such as curry and vegetables. Today, everything is in plastic bags, adding to Thailand's plastic pollution problem. Having received the food, the monk recites a short blessing. In this way, women, who cannot become members of the clergy, receive merit.

RIGHT:

Jetty, Chao Phraya River

This Klong Toey jetty, peaceful and serene, is opposite one of the few undeveloped parts of Bangkok – Bang Ka Chao, nicknamed the 'lungs of Bangkok'. This area of green has been preserved in a bend in the river.

Wat Arun, West Bank of Chao Phraya River
One of the most recognisable symbols of Bangkok is the *prang* (tower) of the Temple of Dawn with its four satellite towers, here silhouetted against the sunset. Although planned by King Taksin (r. 1767–82), it was only completed in the reign of King Rama III (r. 1824–51). The *prang* shape, Khmer in origin and symbolising the abode of the gods, is clad with porcelain tiles.

Northern Thailand

The upper north, bordered by Myanmar (Burma) on the west and Laos on the east, only became part of Thailand in the late 18th century. Until then it was the kingdom of Lanna (13th–18th centuries), which at times was tributary to Burma. As a result, the region developed a distinctive culture, language, art and cuisine. The people of Lanna were also Theravada Buddhists and the region has beautiful northern-style temples, particularly in Chiang Mai and Lampang.

Thailand's highest mountains are in the north and with 34 national parks it is a mecca for trekking, rafting and caving. Densely forested, from the late-19th century, the British negotiated teak concessions using elephants to extract the valuable timber.

Over many, many decades, seven hill tribe groups have migrated from China and Burma: the Akha (80,000), Hmong (150,000), Karen (1,000,000), Lahu (100,000), Lawa (17,000), Lisu (55,000) and Yao (60,000). Living in remote, elevated villages, they practised subsistence agriculture and opium-growing until the mid-20th century, when the government introduced replacement crops. Many are skilled silversmiths and seamstresses.

The lower north, adjoining the central plain in the south and Isaan in the east, centres around the 12th-century capital of Sukhothai-Srisatchanalai, the first Thai kingdom and birthplace of a golden age of Buddhist art and architecture.

OPPOSITE:
Rice Terraces, Mae Chaem, Chiang Mai Province
Although rice remains a dietary staple in the North, as elsewhere in Thailand, the variety grown here is generally glutinous rice, which having only one type of starch becomes sticky when steamed. The name Lanna means 'one million rice fields' and on the steep slopes with heavy rainfall terracing is essential.

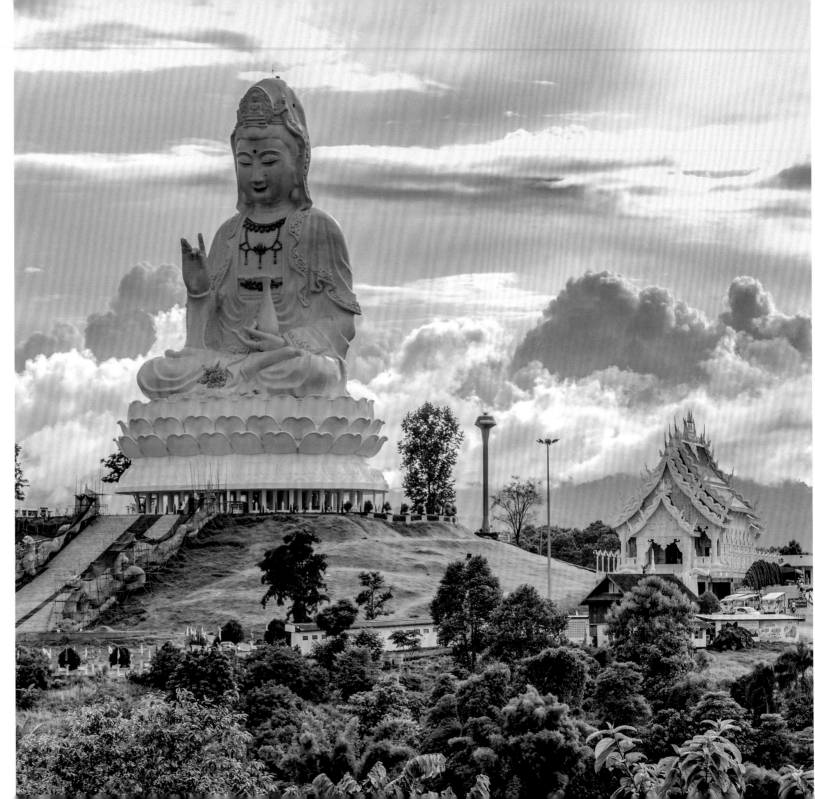

RIGHT:

Guan Im, Wat Huai Pla Kang, Chiang Rai

This recently-built and remarkable image of the bodhisattva of compassion, Guan Im (sometimes mis-identified as the Buddha), is situated just outside Chiang Rai and occupies a commanding hilltop location. An elevator allows visitors to rise up into the bodhisattva's forehead and perhaps gain insight through gazing out over the surrounding landscape.

OPPOSITE:

Fon Lep Traditional Dance, Chiang Rai

One of the classic northern Thai dances is the Fon Lep ('fingernail dance'). Six-inch long brass tubes ending in a sweeping point are worn over the fingers, the dancers' hands having been gently bent back since childhood to create a pleasing arc. The *phasin*, or tube skirt, is typically northern in style, with its alternating bands of dark and light.

ABOVE:

Tea Plantation, Chiang Rai
Although tea-growing in
Thailand may date back
1,000 years, having been
introduced by the southern
Chinese migrations from
Yunnan, commercial tea
plantations, like those for
coffee, date back to the
1980s as part of the opium
eradication programme. The
main tea variety grown in
Chiang Rai is Oolong.

RIGHT:

Doi Chiang Dao
The 2175-metre (7135-ft)
high limestone mountain
is part of the Chiang Dao
Wildlife Sanctuary in Chiang
Mai province and is the third
highest peak in Thailand.
Doi Chiang Dao is a popular
bird-watching site, with
over 300 species recorded,
while in the winter azaleas
and rhododendrons fill the
mountain with colour.

**Umbrella Factory,
Chiang Mai**
Oiled paper umbrellas on
a split bamboo frame have
been made in Chiang Mai for
hundreds of years. The craft
has links with immigrants
from China and with Burma,
which ruled this northern
kingdom for two centuries
between 1558 and 1774. The
centre for umbrella-making is
based around Bor Sang village.
Tourists can also paint their
own umbrellas.

**Coffee Plantations,
Chiang Rai Province**
Formerly, hill tribe villagers
in remote villages in northern
Thailand cultivated opium, a
crop that while lucrative and
non-perishable, is illegal. Over
the past 50 years, Thailand
has become a world leader in
alternative crop replacement,
with coffee proving most
successful. Here, it is harvested
by women from the Akha
tribe (80,000 live in Northern
Thailand).

LEFT:

Akha Hill Tribe Women, Chiang Rai Province
Young Akha women, attired in traditional costumes, survey the rolling hills. The Akha first came to Thailand at the beginning of the 20th century. Hill tribes people are encouraged to wear traditional clothes for tourists, but it is doubtful whether much of the money paid on 'hill tribe tours' actually reaches them. Many hill tribe men and women lack Thai ID cards, making access to higher education and work difficult.

OPPOSITE:

Man Preparing a Thatched Roof, Pae Sang-sun Village
As Akha formerly practised slash-and-burn or subsistence farming, their villagers still retain an air of insubstantiality, although in fact the houses are sturdy and stable. The grass thatch needs replacing every year or so and grass is attached to split bamboo to make panels applied to the wooden frame.

RIGHT:

**Naphamethinidon and
Naphaphonphumisiri
Chedis, Doi Inthanon,
Chiang Mai Province**

These two striking *chedis*
were built in 1987 to honour
the 60th birthdays of the late
King Bhumibol Adulyadej
and five years later for that
of the Queen Mother (in
1992). They are sited near
the summit of Doi Inthanon,
at 2565m (8415ft) Thailand's
highest mountain, and are
part of a long tradition of
siting stupas and Buddha
images on mountains.

OPPOSITE:

**Monks Prepare for Prayer,
Wat Phra That Doi Suthep,
Chiang Mai Province**

Altogether there are some
300,000 Theravada Buddhist
monks in Thailand,
recognisable by their orange
robes and shaven heads.
Monks live in one of over
29,000 temples and assemble
for prayers in the morning
and evening. Doi Suthep
is one of the most revered
temples in Chiang Mai
province, situated on
a hill 15km (9 miles) outside
the city of Chiang Mai.

Lantern Festival, Wat Phra That Doi Suthep, Chiang Mai Province

Legends hold that a temple was founded here in the 14th century to enshrine a Buddha relic brought by a white elephant. The 24-metre (79-ft) golden *chedi*, with a high, redented base, is typical of northern Thai temple architecture. In November, at full moon, when central Thais float small banana-leaf boats for Loy Krathong, in the North lanterns are released in the Yi Peng festival.

Buddha Images, Wat Phra That Doi Suthep, Chiang Mai Province

Mudras, or hand gestures of Buddha images, have different meanings relating either to incidents from his life, or for use in meditation. From left to right: the *Vajrapradama mudra* (self-confidence); middle: although the left hand is not visible, this is most likely the *abhaya mudra* (absence of fear); right: Repelling the Ocean *mudra* (the Buddha stopped a flood).

OPPOSITE:

Sunday Walking Street, Chiang Mai

Everyone loves the market vibe generated by the Sunday walking street, which runs down Ratchadamnoen Road from Tha Pae Gate. Between four p.m. and midnight, visitors can escape the relentless traffic and pick up locally-made craft items such as Lanna-style lacquerware products, teak utensils, T-shirts and much more.

LEFT:

Fish and Seafood Stall, Night Market, Chiang Mai

The Night Bazaar, centred around Loi Khro Road, Chiang Mai, is a must for visitors to the capital of the north, selling handicrafts, textiles, silver, and handmade paper products, as well as delicious food. Note the gilded *nang kwak*, lucky talisman, seated behind the rows of grilled seabass.

LEFT:

**Warorot Market,
Chiang Mai**

Thai signs in Chiang Mai's
largest market, known locally
as Kad Luang (main market),
advertise pork products,
which are the basis of the
city's most popular snacks.
Kaeb moo, or crispy pork
skin, is used to dip in *nam
prik num* (aubergine and
chilli dip), *moo yor* sausage is
sliced into salads. Most Thai
visitors will leave Chiang Mai
with some food souvenirs.

ABOVE:

**Yi Peng Festival, Wat Prathat
Hariphunchai, Lamphun
Province**

Wat Phra That, Hariphunchai,
is one of the most important
temples in northern Thailand,
forming the centre of an early
culture of the same name.
The original stupa dated to
the ninth century underwent
a major renovation in 1443 by
King Tilokaraja. The Yi Peng
lantern festival is held on the
full moon of the twelfth lunar
month, usually in November.

RIGHT:

***Kantoke* Set**

Kantoke refers to a set
meal eaten in northern
Thailand and Laos on special
occasions. Various northern
Thai delicacies are arranged
on a bamboo and red lacquer
tray, which normally is raised
off the ground. Note the
sticky rice in a small woven
basket and the pork skin to
be dipped in *nam prik num*
(lower left).

OPPOSITE:

**Elephant Conservation
Centre, Lampang**

The centre, established in
1993, cares for around 50 or
so elephants, including some
white elephants belonging
to the king. In the past,
elephants were essential to
Thai life, whether in warfare,
for general transportation
and later in extracting teak
from difficult mountainous
forests. A daily ritual at the
centre is taking the elephants
for a bath in the local river.

ABOVE:

Karen Weavers, Doi Inthanon, Chiang Mai Province
The Karen are by far the most numerous of the seven hill
tribes living in Northern Thailand. Women weave using a
traditional back-strap loom. Traditional colours are red,
white and black, although blue is also used, as seen here.
Note the bands of *ikat* weave alternating with the plain red
on the tube skirts of the weavers.

OPPOSITE:

Wat Chaloem Prakiat, Chae Hom, Lampang Province
Located in a national park, the white *chedis*, perching
precariously on vertiginous limestone outcrops, are accessed
by taking a *songtaew* (small pickup truck) and hiking up a
steep trail with 800 steps at the end. Locals believe that there
were Buddha footprints here, hence its previous name, Phu
Phrabat (literally 'Buddha footprint mountain').

Handicrafts, Lanna Folklife Museum, Chiang Mai

Lai rot nam, or gold lacquerware, is a technique in which gold leaf is applied to an adhesive design painted onto wooden or bamboo receptacles coated in black or red lacquer (see top left). The technique was probably introduced from southern China many centuries ago, but its exact origins remain obscure.

Traditionally teak forests, in the early 20th century managed by the British, were plentiful in northern Thailand. Today, even though the wood is no longer abundant, carving animals (lower left) and other artefacts remains an important craft.

As well as *lai rot nam* gold on black lacquer, the deep brick red is a colour very much associated with Lanna and Burmese artefacts (bottom right). Here the swirling vegetal design is more typical of central Thai taste.

RIGHT:

Handmade Umbrella, Chiang Mai

A woman skilfully interweaves strands of coloured cotton round a delicate structure of split bamboo on the underside of a paper umbrella, waxed to resist water.

**Yun Lai Viewpoint, Pai,
Mae Hong Son Province**
This viewpoint with
adjoining café and bungalows
is a favourite spot to catch the
sunrise over fields of flowers
and often layers of mist. The
small town of Pai, formerly
home to ethnic Shan, who
now mainly live in Myanmar,
is near the border. Today it is
a centre for bamboo rafting,
as well as treks to visit hill
tribe villages of the Karen,
Hmong, Lisu and Lahu.

ALL PHOTOGRAPHS:
Wihan Luang, Wat Phra That Lampang Luang, Lampang Province
This Lanna-style temple is a magnificent example of northern Thai Buddhist architecture. The open-sided *wihan luang*, or principal meeting hall, dates to 1476 and is thought to be the oldest wooden structure in Thailand. The triple-tiered wooden roof is supported by massive columns painted black and gold in typical Lanna style. The large, gilded *mondop* in the centre houses a Buddha image cast in 1563.

The principal *chedi* (left), said to enshrine a relic of the Buddha, was built in 1449 and restored in 1496. It is clad in sheets of copper and bronze that over the years have weathered to an unusual colour.

81

***Naga* Staircase, Wat Phra That Lampang Luang, Lampang Province**

Multi-headed *nagas*, their elongated bodies forming stairway balustrades, act as doorway guardians at many Buddhist temples. The *naga*, a mythical snake protecting the treasures of the ocean, have a long association with Buddhism, as it was the *naga* Ananta who protected the Buddha as he meditated before enlightenment. At the top, the tiered doorway is in typical Lanna style.

BOTH PHOTOGRAPHS:

Wat Si Chum, Sukhothai Historical Park

Today the 15-metre (50-ft) high Buddha, known as Phra Achana, sits serenely in the roofless *mandapa* of Wat Si Chum. The iconic image is portrayed in the *Bhumiparsa mudra*, or the moment when the long, tapering fingers of the Buddha's right hand touch the earth to signify his attainment of enlightenment, hence the name 'Calling the Earth to Witness' *mudra*.

The name of the image is known from an inscription found at the temple, which also provided important information about the founding of Sukhothai. The gold leaf on the image's right hand has been applied by devotees over the years.

RIGHT:

Wat Sa Si, Sukhothai Historical Park

The heavily restored Buddha image on the ruined *viharn* platform of Wat Sa Si is also seated in the *bhumisparsa mudra*, the most common portrayal in Thai Buddhist art. The laterite columns, created by digging up locally-found iron-rich clay which hardens when dry, would have been coated with many layers of stucco.

OPPOSITE:

Wat Mahathat, Sukhothai Historical Park

Inscribed as a UNESCO world heritage site in 1991, Sukhothai is situated in a fertile plain surrounded by hills. Wat Mahathat, or Great Relic Temple, stands at the centre of the city, its bell-shaped stupa inspired by Sri Lankan models. Originally, the prayer halls, identifiable by laterite columns, would have had wooden and tiled roofs. Subsidiary stupas enshrine the relics of revered monks or dignitaries.

Loy Kratong Festival, Wat Mahathat, Sukhothai Historical Park

Sukhothai is regarded as Thailand's first capital, existing from 1238–1438, following liberation from the Khmer empire. Its most famous king, Ramkhamhaeng (r. 1279–99), is revered as a just ruler, a reviver of Theravada Buddhism and the creator of the Thai alphabet. Allegedly, the Loy Krathong festival of floating lights down river for good luck also originated here.

Northeast Thailand

Northeast Thailand, known to Thais as Isaan (transliterated in multiple ways), is Thailand's largest region (160,000 sq kilometres/61,776 sq miles), comprising 20 provinces centred on the Khorat plateau. It is bordered by the Mekong river to the north and east and Cambodia in the lower east, with the central plain on the west.

Isaan people have a strong identity and are a potent force politically. Feeling somewhat separate from central Thais, they share more culturally with the Lao. Although the central Thai language is used in education and officialdom, most inhabitants speak a variant of Lao, with Khmer common in the provinces bordering Cambodia.

It is from Isaan that such popular foods as *som tum* and *laab* originated, eaten with sticky rice, while the region's favourite curry, *kaeng paa* (jungle curry) is made without coconut milk and is very spicy. Thailand's country music, *mor lam*, and *look thung*, celebrating the hard life of farmers in this the country's poorest region, comes from here. The poverty of the region drives many young people to find work in Bangkok as labourers, taxi drivers and in the entertainment industry. In the past, during breaks in the agricultural cycle, women would keep silk worms and weave beautiful ikat silks. Silk-weaving villages are still found today.

The northeast has numerous prehistoric settlements, while from the 6th–14th centuries the plateau formed the western side of the Khmer empire centred on Angkor. The ruins of important Khmer temples remain impressive sites today. The region also has 26 national parks, with the most famous being Khao Yai and Phu Kradueng.

OPPOSITE:
Elephants, Chang Village, Ban Ta Klang, Surin
During the Ayutthaya period (1351–1767), when wild elephants roamed the forests and were used in combat and as the mount of kings, round-ups were held annually. The best specimens were brought to Ayutthaya for selection and training, in an event that was a popular spectacle. Today, Surin is an elephant centre and here in Ban Ta Klang village mahouts of the indigenous Kuy tribe train elephants in the traditional way.

LEFT:

**Erawan Cave Mountain,
Nong Bua Lamphu Province**
The limestone mountain
containing one of Thailand's
largest caves rises vertically
from the surrounding wet rice
fields. From certain angles
the mountain resembles an
elephant's head, hence the
name Erawan, after Indra's
three-headed elephant.
The brightest green fields
are rice nursery beds,
nurturing the seedlings
before they are transplanted
by hand into fields filled with
water and mud – a back-
breaking exercise.

OPPOSITE:

**Phi Ta Khon Festival,
Dan Sai, Loei Province**
The three-day festival,
comprises a ghost procession
on the first day, shown here, a
rocket festival on the second
and a third day with chanting
by Buddhist monks. Although
linked with Buddhism, the
festival also seeks protection
from Phra Upakut, the spirit
of the Mun river.

ALL PHOTOGRAPHS:

Erawan Cave, Na Wang, Nong Bua Lamphu Province
The large limestone cave, with some impressive stalactites and stalagmites, is reached by over 600 steps, making the cool interior a welcome relief after the long climb.

The forest-monk tradition in Northeast Thailand is an ancient one, in which monks leave the monastic life of large temples for solitary retreats in caves. There, through concentrated meditation, they hope to achieve nirvana (a cessation of the endless cycle of birth and rebirth). Caves of renowned practitioners become pilgrimage sites for devotees who install images of the Buddha and small shrines.

The large image of the Buddha (left), recently painted gold, is just visible from below.

**Pha Mak Duk Cliff,
Phu Kradueng National
Park, Loei Province**
In 1962, Phu Kradueng
National Park was the second
park to be established in
Thailand after Khao Yai.
The roughly square plateau
rises abruptly some 1250
metres (4100ft) from the
surrounding plain. Forest
succession is easily observable
as one climbs the 11.2km
(7 mile) path to the top,
where camping is possible
in designated areas. The
diverse vegetation supports
a fauna of elephants, bears,
deer, gibbons, macaques
and smaller mammals,
while the sandstone cliffs
provide stunning views of the
surrounding plain.

Prasat Hin Phanom Rung, Burirum Province

The Hindu temple of Phanom Rung, built between the 10th and 13th centuries when the Khmer empire extended west from Angkor into present-day Thailand, is sited at 400m (1300ft) on the rim of an extinct volcano. A 160-metre (520-ft) processional walkway ends in steps and *naga* terraces leading to the temple proper. Built of sandstone, the temple with a tall *prang* (central tower) symbolising Mount Meru is beautifully carved with lintels and pediments depicting the Hindu gods.

ABOVE:

Umamahesvara Lintel, Muang Tam, Burirum Province

Nearby and below Phanom Rung lies the Hindu temple
of Muang Tam, meaning 'low city'. Five *prangs* (towers)
stand on a low base, surrounded with four ponds. The
deeply carved sandstone lintel shows the god Shiva and
his wife Uma riding on the bull Nandin, above a *kala* face,
surrounded by an elaborate garland.

OPPOSITE:

**Shiva Nataraja Pediment, Phanom Rung,
Burirum Province**

Above the main entrance to the central tower is this beautiful
representation of a dancing Shiva. Shiva is the most
important among the *Trimurti* (triumvirate) of Hindu gods,
followed by Vishnu and Brahma. Shiva, as Lord of the Dance,
acts to both create and destroy.

LEFT:

Traditional Float, Bun Bang Fai Festival, Yasothon, Yasothon Province

While today this Lao festival is linked with Buddhist merit-making, it is believed to derive from pre-Buddhist fertility festivals held to encourage the beginning of the monsoon rains so vital for rice planting. After two days of processions, dancing, *mor lam* music and alcohol, the festival culminates on day three with the rocket-firing competition.

ABOVE:

Laab* and *Som Tum

Laab, finely-chopped pork or chicken mixed with chilli, lime, roasted rice and herbs, and *som tum*, unripe papaya salad flavoured with chilli, lime, garlic and peanuts, are emblematic of Isaan food. Eaten with sticky rice and often grilled chicken, over the past two decades the popularity of *som tum* has spread worldwide.

103

Wat Non Kum, Nakhon Ratchasima Province
This modern temple was completed in 2000 to house an enormous image of Luang Por Toh, one of Thailand's most revered monks, who after years meditating gained a huge following.

The classical Thai architecture reflects in the pond and is a symbol of the enduring power of Theravada Buddhism in Thailand. It was funded by a famous actor, Sorapong Chatree.

OPPOSITE:
Prasat Hin Phimai, Nakhon Ratchasima Province
The central tower of the Khmer sanctuary soars above the surrounding gallery and is flanked by two towers, sandstone on the west and laterite on the east. Built and added to from the 10th to 13th centuries, Phimai combines Hindu and later Buddhist iconography. Standing on the royal road to Angkor, it is unusually oriented south towards the Khmer capital. The entrance causeway is laterite, while the central tower is sandstone.

LEFT:
Gateways, Prasat Hin Phimai, Nakhon Ratchasima Province
One of the characteristics of Khmer architecture is copying in sandstone the forms and appearance of wood turning. Thus, the columns and inner frames of the various doorways are carved to imitate wood. The enclosure walls are laterite, which was less expensive and could be dug up locally from the clay soil, rich in decomposed stone and iron.

Sai Ngam (Banyan Tree), Phimai, Nakhon Ratchasima Province

This banyan grove, possibly over 300 years old, covers an area of 1,350 sq metres (14,500 sq ft). Banyan trees send tendrils into the ground, which develop roots and create new trees. Eventually the original tree can no longer be identified. Believing that female spirits inhabit such trees, visitors make offerings at the spirit house, before tucking into *som tum* and fried chicken and perhaps having their fortunes told.

OPPOSITE:

Mekong River, Nong Khai

At 4,350km (2,700 miles), the Mekong River is the longest river in Southeast Asia, running through six countries. For 850km (528 miles) it forms the border between Thailand and Laos. Home to the rare Irrawaddy dolphin and the giant catfish, both now endangered, dams and dredging by China have severely impacted the river's ecology and flow, as well as the livelihoods of local fishermen and farmers.

TOP AND BOTTOM LEFT:

Silk Weaving, Ban Rae, Khwao Sinarin District, Surin

Traditionally, after the rice harvest, Isaan women would spin and weave silk underneath their wooden houses on stilts. Silk worms (*Bombyx mori*) are fed on mulberry leaves for several weeks, before they spin silk cocoons. After three days the worm is killed to keep the silk filaments intact. The silk is then spun on a wheel before weaving. Although commercial dyes are often used, complex *ikat* patterns are still employed (see bottom left).

Western and Central Thailand

The six provinces of western Thailand run down the border with Myanmar from the mountainous forests of Tak and Kamphaeng Phet in the north to the narrow strip of Prachuap Khiri Khun in the south, home to the popular seaside resorts of Cha-am and Hua Hin. The region has some of the country's most beautiful national parks, such as Kaeng Krachan and Khao Sam Roi Yod, while Kanchanaburi province was the site of the notorious 'Death Railway' built by prisoners of war under the Japanese during World War II.

To the east, the western region joins with the central region, which comprises provinces within the alluvial flood plain of the Chao Phraya river (literally 'Lord of the Rivers'). The river begins in Nakhon Sawan at the confluence of the Ping and Nan rivers to flow 590 kilometres (372 miles) south into the Gulf of Thailand. At the heart of central Thailand is Bangkok, the capital city, but some 700 years earlier, the capital of Ayutthaya also arose in the Central Plain in 1350 and Siam became a great mercantile centre visited by Chinese and Muslim traders and the first Europeans. Today, the ruins of Ayutthaya are a UNESCO world heritage site.

During the 19th century, central Thailand was developed for rice growing. Today, rice is grown throughout the country (Thailand is the world's second biggest rice exporter), but the area north of Bangkok has become an industrial centre with easy access to airports and ports.

OPPOSITE:
Fishing Boat, Hua Hin, Prachuap Khiri Khan Province
Once a sleepy fishing village, Hua Hin was first developed as a seaside retreat by members of the Thai royal family in the early 20th century after the railway station opened in 1911. One of Thailand's earliest resort hotels in European style (now the Sofitel) opened in 1922 and a golf course followed shortly. Today, the town has grown extensively and has a large ex-pat population attracted by the seafood, climate and relatively cheap lifestyle.

OVERLEAF:
Fishing Boats, Hua Hin, Prachuap Khiri Khan Province
Despite overfishing in the Gulf of Thailand, fishermen still go out in small boats, often at night, when their boats, festooned with green fluorescent lights to attract squid, glow eerily on the horizon.

ABOVE:

Phraya Nakhon Cave, Khao Sam Roi Yod, Prachuap Khiri Khan Province
Phraya Nakhon Cave is a magical destination reached via a 400-metre (1300-ft) steep climb up from Laem Sala beach. King Chulalongkorn visited the cave in 1890 and the pavilion seen today was built in his honour. The hole in the ceiling allows sunlight to penetrate, illuminating the pavilion at certain times of year.

RIGHT:

Khao Sam Roi Yod, Prachuap Khiri Khan Province
The park's name, meaning 'Mountains with 300 summits', aptly describes the sea of limestone peaks rising vertically from the plain. Established in 1966 as Thailand's first marine park and covering 98 sq kilometres (38 sq miles), the park includes the location where King Mongkut (r. 1851–1868) invited officials and foreign dignitaries to view a total solar eclipse in August 1868.

LEFT:

Fishing Boat, Cha-am Beach, Phetchaburi Province
Facing west across the gulf of Thailand, spectacular sunsets are a regular treat. Developed slightly later than Hua Hin, Cha-am preserves a more relaxed, laid-back atmosphere. Easy to reach from Bangkok, the resort is as popular with Thai beachgoers as foreigners.

OVERLEAF LEFT:

Bang Kao village, Cha-am Beach, Phetchaburi Province
The trees silhouetted against the sunset are sugar palms, not coconuts. The region around Phetchaburi is famous for the desserts made with palm sugar, *khanom moh kaeng* (a caramel custard made with coconut). Palm sugar is also an essential ingredient of *kaeng kiew waan* (green curry with *waan* meaning 'sweet').

OVERLEAF RIGHT:

Thailand International Kite Festival, Cha-am Beach, Phetchaburi Province
Since 2000 the international kite festival, held annually in March, attracts kiters from all around the world. Thailand has a centuries-old tradition of kite flying in the breezy, hot season of March and April. In the past, competitions were held on Sanam Luang, the open area outside the Grand Palace, Bangkok, with King Chulalongkorn being a fan of the sport.

Phra Nakhon Khiri Palace, Phetchaburi
Situated on three small hills above the town of Phetchaburi, the group comprising a palace, temple and observatory, known locally as *khao wang* (literally 'palace hill'), was built as a summer abode by King Mongkut (r. 1851–68) in 1860. The king was a keen amateur astronomer and included an observatory to look at the night sky.

Kaeng Krachan National Park, Phetchaburi Province

At almost 3,000 sq kilometres (1160 sq miles), this is the largest national park in Thailand. It was established in 1981 and runs along the Burmese border on its western side. The dam on the Phetchaburi river from which the park takes its name was built in 1969. Ninety-one species of mammals and 461 bird varieties have been recorded in the park.

THIS PAGE, CLOCKWISE FROM TOP LEFT:

Kaeng Krachan National Park Wildlife

Dusky leaf monkeys (*Trachypithecus obscurus*) are also known as spectacled langurs for the white rings around their eyes.

So far 63 reptile species have been recorded here, but there are likely to be many more. Emma Gray's forest lizard (*Calotes emma*) is also known as the crested forest lizard. It is found throughout mainland Southeast Asia.

The Eurasian hoopoe (*Upupa epops*) has a pan-Eurasian distribution and is easily identifiable from its distinctive crown of feathers.

Thailand has more than 200 snake species and Kaeng Krachan is home to many of them, including the common keelback snake (*Xenochrophis flavipunctatus*).

**Erawan Waterfall,
Erawan National Park,
Kanchanaburi Province**
The waterfall is named after
the three-headed elephant of
Hindu mythology, Airavata
(Erawan in Thai), mount of
the god Indra, as the effect
created by the cascades is
said to resemble an elephant's
head. The waterfall is located
in the Tenessarim hills on the
border with Burma.

**Death Railway,
Kanchanaburi Province**
The railway, so-called because
about 90,000 Southeast Asian
civilian labourers and over
12,000 British and Australian
prisoners of war died in
brutal conditions between
1942 and 1945 during the
Japanese occupation of
Thailand, ran for 415km (258
miles) from Kanchanaburi to
Burma. The plan was to avoid
the dangerous ship passage
around the Malay Peninsula
and link with existing
railways in Burma. It was
closed in 1947 but a section
still runs today between Nong
Pla Tuk and Nam Tok. There
is an excellent visitor centre
at Nam Tok where sections
of the line can be walked,
and a moving museum in
Kanchanaburi town.

ABOVE:

Green Chicken Curry
This ubiquitous Thai curry,
if made correctly, is truly
delicious. It comprises many
ingredients: chicken (or
a different meat or tofu),
coconut milk, curry paste
(chillis, garlic, shallots,
lemongrass, ginger, coriander
leaves and roots), kaffir lime
leaves, pea aubergines, round
aubergines, finger chillies,
palm sugar and Thai holy
basil to give the green tone.

RIGHT:

**Man and Buffalo, Khwae
Noi River, Kanchanaburi
Province**
In the past, the water buffalo
(Bubalus bubalis) was a
vital part of Thai farming,
used for ploughing rice
fields, pulling carts, turning
threshing machines and also
for meat. Recently, numbers
have declined to around
one million as mechanical
ploughs have taken over.

RIGHT AND OPPOSITE:

**Floating Markets,
Amphawa, Samut
Songkhram Province
and Damnoen Saduak,
Ratchaburi Province**

Until the mid-20th century,
transport and trade in
Thailand was waterborne
and settlements developed
along rivers and canals.
Fresh fruit and vegetables
were transported by water
from the orchards around
Bangkok and sold from small
boats by women wearing
ngorb, wide-brimmed
pandanus-leaf hats. While
women remain the principal
market traders, today most
markets are land based.

Both Amphawa (right)
and Damnoen Saduak
(opposite), within easy reach
of Bangkok, are largely aimed
at tourists, but nevertheless
they are a lot of fun and
give a wonderful feel for a
vanished lifestyle.

LEFT:

Khao Ngu Stone Park, Ratchaburi Province

A clever local initiative has converted an old limestone quarry into a visitor attraction near the town of Ratchaburi. It is located within a typical Thai karst landscape and gets its name *ngu*, meaning snake, from the sinuous shape of the hill.

OPPOSITE:

Tham Reussi, Khao Ngu Stone Park

The most important aspect of the site are the ancient caves with carvings from the Dvaravati period (6th–11th centuries CE), when Theravada Buddhism became prevalent in what is now central Thailand, leaving evidence in the form of brick stupas, Buddha images and *sema* stones (boundary markers). The large standing Buddha, the missing arms likely in the *abahaya mudra*, projects an aura of serenity.

OVERLEAF:

Khlong Lan National Park, Khampaeng Phet Province

Khlong Lan was declared the 44th of Thailand's now 147 national parks in December 1985. Its forested mountains, covering 300 sq kilometres (116 sq miles), connect to the 1485-metre (4872-ft) peak of Khun Khlong Lan.

LEFT:

**Reclining Buddha,
Wat Lokayasutharam,
Ayutthaya Historical Park**
The many temple ruins in the
historical park, a UNESCO
world heritage site since
1991, reflect the importance
of Thailand's former capital
from 1351 to 1767. With
almost a million inhabitants
at its height, Ayutthaya was
a major trading centre until
sacked by the Burmese.
The 42-metre (138-ft) long
reclining Buddha in the *para
nirvana* posture is often
covered with a yellow or
orange robe.

ABOVE:

**Wat Chai Wattanaram,
Ayutthaya Historical Park**
The temple with a Khmer-
style central tower was built
by King Prasart Thong of
Ayutthaya in 1630 outside
the main island of Ayutthaya
city. In 1431, the Thais had
invaded Cambodia, making it
a vassal, and the Khmer style
became popular. The plan
reflects Buddhist cosmology:
the central *prang* represents
Mount Meru, surrounded by
eight smaller *chedis*.

RIGHT:

Buddha Head, Wat Mahathat, Ayutthaya Historical Park

A Buddha head, with an enigmatic gaze, entrapped in the clutches of a ficus tree, has become almost emblematic of Ayutthaya. According to the Thai chronicles, the first temple on the site was built by King Barommaracha I in 1374. Its name, Mahathat – Great Relic – indicates the temple housed a Buddha relic in the central *prang*.

OPPOSITE:

Wat Phra Si Sanphet, Ayutthaya Historical Park

Once the location of the royal palace, the site was transformed into a temple in 1448. In 1492, in the reign of King Ramathibodi II, two tall, bell-shaped *chedis* were built for the ashes of his father and brother, with a third added in 1532. As a royal temple, it was used exclusively for ceremonies. The *chedis* were restored after World War II.

LEFT:

Elephant, Khao Yai National Park, Nakhon Nayok Province

Khao Yai is Thailand's oldest and best-known national park, established in 1962 and covering an area of 300 sq kilometres (116 sq miles). Recently development of the surrounding area, popular with Bangkokians for its cooler climate and pure air, has caused problems for animal conservation. The park is one of the few places that is home to wild elephants, and cars must remain stationary when they wander down the road.

RIGHT:

Dark Blue Tiger Butterflies, Kaeng Krachan National Park

May and June in Kaeng Krachan are the best months and the best place for butterfly spotting, with some 300 species recorded in the park. Here blue tiger butterflies (*Tirumala septentionis*) are 'puddling', namely sipping moisture from the earth.

ALL PHOTOGRAPHS:
Monkeys, Prang Sam Yod, Lopburi
The Mahayana Buddhist temple of Prang Sam Yod (meaning
'three prangs', or towers) dates to the reign of the Khmer king
Jayavarman VII (r. 1181–1221) and is in the Bayon style of that
king's state temple at Angkor.

Originally a statue of Buddha under Naga was installed
in the centre, with the bodhisattvas Avalokiteshvara and
Prajnaparamita on either side. At that time Lopburi was an
important regional centre, and even sent tribute missions
to China. Today, the temple is inhabited by hundreds of
macaques who can be quite aggressive. An annual Monkey
Festival takes place at the end of November.

ABOVE:

Monks on the Morning Alms Round, Chainat Province
Around 6.00 a.m. every day, except in the rainy season, after an hour of meditation and chanting, monks make their morning alms round. Local people have an opportunity to gain merit by presenting food, which is taken to the monastery and eaten before midday. Here, they walk along the small earthen dyke, or bund, separating the recently planted rice fields.

RIGHT:

Rice Fields
Rice, the staple diet of Thailand, has been grown here for several thousand years. Wet rice farming is labour intensive, with seedlings nurtured in nursery beds (here showing the brightest green) and then transplanted by hand. Traditionally, planting happens during the rainy season, with harvest time from November to December.

Although the introduction of new rice varieties has made two or even three annual crops possible, the accompanying need for fertiliser and pesticides makes farmers dependent on outside merchants.

RIGHT:
Standing Buddha Statue, Wat Phra Borommathat Wora Wihan, Chainat Province

The temple dates to the Ayutthaya period (1351–1767). The main image is known as Luangpho Thammachak, a standing Buddha in the *ham yad* posture, 'Persuading relatives not to quarrel'. The image is flanked by a portrait of Queen Sirikit the Queen Mother and HM King Vajiralongkorn, thereby combining two pillars of Thai society – Buddhism and the monarchy.

OPPOSITE:
Buddhist Monks, Makha Bucha Day, Wat Phra Dhammakaya, Pathum Thani Province

The important Buddhist festival of Makha Bucha is celebrated in the third lunar month, February or March, to commemorate the day when the Buddha preached his first sermon to 1250 monks who arrived together without prior arrangement. Such festivals are particularly impressive at this enormous temple just north of Don Muang airport.

150

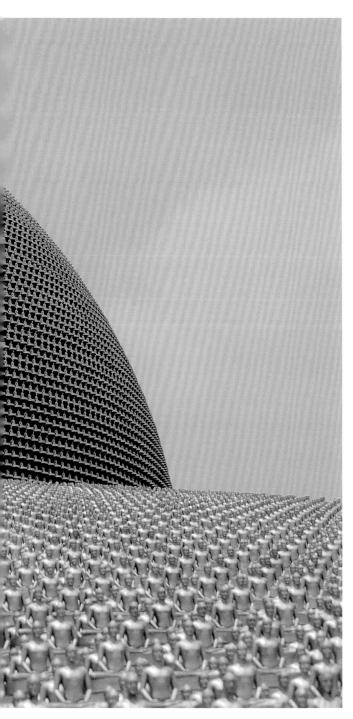

BOTH PHOTOGRAPHS:

Golden Buddha Figurines, Wat Phra Dhammakaya, Pathum Thani Province

Believed to be the largest temple in the world, Wat Phra Dhammakaya, established in 1970, is the main monastery of the Dhammakaya sect, founded early in the 20th century. On a plot of 320 hectares, its 150 buildings give traditional Buddhist concepts modern form. Its success in attracting some three million adherents worldwide has led to accusations by the government of corruption and cult-like behaviour.

An estimated 300,000 small Buddha images combine to create the futuristic dome of the central *chedi*.

Giant Three-headed Elephant, Erawan Museum, Samut Prakan Province

The fantastical brain-child of visionary businessman Lek Viriyaphant (1914–2000), the temple-museum is housed within a giant, three-headed elephant, Erawan, mount of the god Indra. The exuberant bronze statue is 29 metres (95ft) high with a 15-metre (49-ft) high pedestal.

Interior Ceiling, Erawan Museum, Samut Prakan Province

The interior reflects Hindu and Buddhist cosmological beliefs: the lower floor, within the pedestal, represents the Underworld and houses a collection of Ming and Qing dynasty vases; the second floor, the human realm, showcases more ceramics and European porcelain; the third floor, symbolising Tavatimsa heaven atop Mount Meru, displays Buddha relics and images.

Eastern Thailand

Geographically smaller than the other regions, eastern Thailand is one of extremes. Its seven provinces stretch from the Gulf of Thailand in the west to the Cambodian border (Sa Kaeo, Chanthaburi and Trat provinces) in the east. The industrialism of the eastern seaboard development (Chachoengsao, Chonburi and Rayong provinces), with the port of Laem Chabang and its associated petrochemical industry, contrasts with the relaxed beach resorts in the east. This is the region where most visitors arrive in Thailand, as it is also home to Suvarnabhumi airport, opened in 2006. Nearby is the notorious seaside resort of Pattaya, which during the Vietnam War developed as a centre for American GIs to enjoy 'R and R', rest and recreation. Today, Pattaya has become a sprawling cosmopolitan city with hotels, malls and seedier bars.

Despite urbanization to the west, the east of this region has some important national parks, such as the 844 kilometre-square (325 sq miles) Pang Sida (Sa Kaeo province), which forms part of the Dong Phayayen-Khao Yai UNESCO forest complex, and over 85 per cent of the island of Ko Chang to the far south, where the marine park provides superb opportunities for diving and snorkelling.

Finally, if you fancy yourself as a gem connoisseur, a visit to Chanthaburi's weekend gem market may prove either a wonderful bargain or a costly mistake.

OPPOSITE:
Ko Kut, Trat Province
With its coconut palm and mangrove-fringed shoreline, white sands and clear sea, Ko Kut embodies many elements of a tropical paradise. Situated on the east of the Gulf of Thailand, near the Cambodian border, its distance from Bangkok (a four-hour drive, or short flight and then a 30-minute boat ride) have helped to keep the island largely unspoiled.

Fish Farm, Gulf of Thailand
Thailand has long been a major fishing nation, with a coastline of 2600km (1,615 miles) and waters of 319,750 sq kilometres (123,456 sq miles). Recently fish stocks have been declining and fish farming in cages by the coast has increased. The main fish farmed is tilapia.

157

LEFT:

Prasae Mangrove, Rayong Province

Unlike the picture postcard fantasy of swaying palm trees and white sand beaches, the Gulf of Thailand was originally ringed with mangrove forests, whose stilt roots are adapted for tidal areas, create nursery beds for fish and prawns and protect the coastline from erosion. Destruction of mangroves for charcoal-making and prawn farming has made this site of 10 square kilometres (3.8 sq miles) particularly important.

OPPOSITE:

Khao Laem Ya-Mu Ko Samet National Park, Rayong Province

The small, 131-sq-kilometre (50-sq-mile) park covers Ko Samet and neighbouring small islands. In 2013, three illegally-built resorts which had encroached on the park were destroyed, but the island still has an active tourist scene on one side of the island, with a quieter atmosphere on the other. Being close to Bangkok makes it popular with both Thai and foreign visitors.

Fire Show, Ko Samet, Rayong Province
After dinner in one of the many restaurants lining the beaches of Sai Kaew and Ao Phai, fire shows are a constant thrill for the many tourists, both domestic and foreign, who lounge on the sand at small tables to enjoy buckets of cocktails.

LEFT:
Kai Bae Beach, Ko Chang, Trat Province
This is one of the more peaceful beaches on Thailand's third largest island, near the Cambodian border, which until the 1980s was almost completely undeveloped. Named Elephant Island, from its shape like the head of an elephant, the highest peak, Khao Salak, reaches 744 metres (2440ft). Smaller nearby islands provide excellent snorkelling and diving.

ABOVE:
Buddhist Monk, Ko Chang, Trat Province
An elderly Buddhist monk takes a break on the small terrace outside his *kuti*, or residence. On the table behind is one of the few things monks are allowed to own – his alms bowl with which to make the morning round for food. Also in evidence are several orange buckets used by devotees to make donations of useful household items at the monastery.

LEFT:

Super One Race 2014, Bira International Circuit, Chonburi Province

The circuit, opened in 1988, was named after the Thai prince, Prince Birabongse Bhanubandh, who in the 1930s rose to international fame as a racing driver in Britain and Europe under the management of his cousin, Prince Chula Chakrabongse. The 2.41km (1.5 mile) circuit is unfortunately too short for Formula 1, but many other races, including Superbike Racing, take place here.

OPPOSITE:

Pla Tu (Mackerel), Samut Prakan Province

Thai mackerel, presented here in round bamboo baskets, breed and live in the Gulf of Thailand. Five rivers enter the Gulf and the mix of fresh and salt water creates abundant plankton for the mackerel fry. Nevertheless, declining fish stocks have meant the delicacy is no longer cheap. Mackerel is generally eaten fried with a dipping sauce and rice, or in spicy salads and soups.

Pattaya, Chonburi Province
The city at night. Pattaya was a sleepy fishing village with a beautiful beach until the 1960s and the knock-on effects of the Vietnam War changed everything. Over the past 50 years it has developed into a 24-hour city with condos, hotels, clubs, shows and menus in at least six languages.

Boat Races, Mabprachan Lake, Pattaya, Chonburi Province
Once a year in November, teams from Vietnam, Cambodia and Laos get together on this 10-kilometre (6.5-mile)-long reservoir near Pattaya to compete in long-boat races, one of many festivals held here, including Loy Krathong and buffalo racing. Thailand has a long tradition of long-boat racing held after the end of the Buddhist annual rains retreat (*Vassa*) in October.

OPPOSITE:

Mixed Deciduous Forest,
Ta Phraya National Park,
Sa Kaeo Province
The 594-sq-kilometre
(229-sq-miles) park, part
of the Phnom Dongrak
mountain range, was
established in 1996 near the
Cambodia border in an area
formerly housing refugee
camps as a result of the war
in Vietnam and Cambodia.
As well as diverse fauna,
including three types of deer,
sun bears, gibbons, palm
civet, gaur and rare birds, the
park has some Khmer ruins.

LEFT:

Wat Buppharam,
Trat Province
Known locally as Wat Plai
Klong ('Temple at the End of
the Canal'), the oldest temple
in Trat was founded in 1652
during the Ayutthaya period.
It is important for the ancient
wooden *viharn* (assembly
hall) with its well-preserved
and unrestored murals. There
is also a collection of wooden
oxcarts and more modern
concrete sculptures warning
against licentious behaviour.

LEFT:
Fisherman, Bang Phra Lake, Chonburi Province
The lake is one of 52 Non-Hunting Areas in Thailand where locals are allowed to fish but hunting birds and mammals is forbidden. Ringed with grassland with woodland behind, the lake supports a diverse and changing bird population. On a good day over 100 species can be spotted, including quail and storks.

OPPOSITE:
Ban Nam Chiao, Trat Province
This community of Buddhist and Muslim fishermen working together harmoniously is about 8km (5 miles) from Trat town. The original Buddhist inhabitants were joined by Cham and Malay Muslims fleeing persecution in the mid-19th century. Today, visitors can go fishing with the villagers, learn to cook the daily catch and make the hats for which the community is famous.

RIGHT:

Jetty, Ko Kut, Trat Province
Ko Kut is Thailand's fifth
largest island at 25km
(15 miles) long and 12km
(7 miles) wide, but, with
a population of less than
2500, is far less spoilt than
the big three (Phuket, Samui,
Ko Chang), and provides
a wonderful mix of forest,
waterfalls, sandy beaches and
sunsets. Unlike Ko Chang,
there is no car ferry, so
visitors rent scooters or hire
small boats.

BOTH PHOTOGRAPHS:

**Ko Si Chang,
Chonburi Province**

In the late 19th century, this was where King Chulalongkorn (r. 1868–1910) built Chudhadhuj Palace to escape the heat of Bangkok. After the French used it as a base to attack Bangkok in 1893, the palace was abandoned, but the site retains a melancholic charm. A climb to the hilltop Golden Buddha gives a commanding view of the boat-filled harbour. Various caves named after the former royal inhabitants, such as Tham Saowabha and Tham Chakrabongse, house Buddha images or provide refuge for meditating monks.

Wing Kwai Water Buffalo Racing Festival, Chonburi Province

The week-long annual festival, held for over 140 years, takes place in the 11th lunar month, usually October. The normally placid buffalo train rigorously beforehand and achieve quite a turn of speed, driving the crowds to a frenzy. As well as racing, competitions include most comically-dressed and best-dressed buffalo, so if you can't be fast, be eye-catching.

OVERLEAF:

Pang Sida Waterfall, Pang Sida National Park, Sa Kaeo Province

Pang Sida National Park forms part of the Dong Phaya Yen-Khao Yai mountain complex near the Cambodian border. The 10-metre waterfall cascades all year round, but is at its most resplendent in the rainy season. Over the years the park has suffered from poachers seeking rare Siamese Rosewood, which in 2013 was selling in China for US$95,000 per cubic metre.

Southern Thailand

outhern Thailand, bordered in the north by the Kra Isthmus and in the south by Malaysia, includes two of Thailand's most popular seaside destinations – Phuket Island, on the west in the Andaman Sea, and Samui Island, on the east in the Gulf of Thailand. It was the west coast that was severely affected by the 2004 tsunami, although little evidence remains today. The population of the three southernmost provinces of Yala, Pattani and Narathiwat is mainly Muslim and ethnically Malay, with a distinct culture and food. Intermittent terrorist acts occur in an attempt to force secession from Thailand. The region was a centre of early human settlement and trade between east and west and the Malay archipelago, with early kingdoms including Tambralinga and Srivijaya. During the Sukhothai (1238–1438) and then Ayutthaya (1350–1767) periods, Nakhon Si Thammarat, site of the region's most important Buddhist temple, became a tribute state.

Several mountain ranges run down the peninsula and heavy erosion of the limestone hills has created dramatic karst formations. Areas submerged at the end of the last ice age formed islands such as Ko Phi Phi and the 'James Bond island' of Phang Nga. There are over 40 national parks, but over-exploitation and unchecked coastal development has led to problems.

OPPOSITE:
Long-tail Fishing Boats, Ao Nang, Krabi Province
Ao Nang forms the centre of the coastal part of Krabi province. While some tourists swim here, many take one of the long-tail boats to other more deserted beaches. A road separates the diverse hotels, restaurants and massage parlours from the beach, ensuring that it remains open access for all. Sunsets along the long strip can be spectacular.

LEFT:

Bansamchong Tai Fishing Village, Phang Nga Bay
Situated on a mangrove-fringed canal, the village of Bansamchong, inhabited by Muslim fishermen and their families, can only be accessed by boat. The villagers' houses are built on stilts and connected by wooden walkways. In the aftermath of the 2004 tsunami, which luckily did not affect them, they decided to begin offering homestays. In the morning, the villages go to inspect the nets cast the night before.

OVERLEAF BOTH PHOTOGRAPHS:
Ao Phang Nga National Park, Phang Nga Province
At the edge of the so-called 'James Bond Island', made famous by the movie *The Man with the Golden Gun*, is the karst tower rising like a giant stalagmite from the sea. The 400 sq-kilometres (154 sq miles) Ao Phang Nga National Marine Park was established in 1981 and compromises over 40 Andaman Sea islands with vertical cliffs, caves and extensive mangroves.

An aerial view of Ao Phang Nga National Park shows in the foreground the primary mangrove forests which are Thailand's most extensive. Behind, some of the sheer karst formations hide caves only accessible at low tide, which make the area particularly enticing for sea kayakers.

RIGHT:

Full Moon Party, Hat Rin Beach, Ko Phang-ngan

Hat Rin is a peninsula with two beaches, 'Sunrise' and 'Sunset'. It has gained notoriety for the full moon parties held every month, when thousands of tourists come to dance and drink themselves senseless. Danny Boyle featured Ko Phang-ngan is his film *The Beach* based on Alex Garland's novel of the same name.

OPPOSITE:

Guanyin Statue, Wat Plai Laem, Ko Samui, Surat Thani Province

The trend for creating giant, sacred images is a feature of 21st-century Thailand, with temples almost vying to outdo each other. In this temple, completed in 2004, a gigantic image of an 18-armed Guanyin – bodhisattva of compassion – in Chinese style, is paired with a 30-metre (98-ft) image of Budai, the Chinese Laughing Buddha.

ABOVE:

Hornbill, Khao Sok National Park, Surat Thani Province
Nine of the world's 57 hornbill species live in Khao Sok National Park, with the greater hornbill being the park's largest bird. Easily recognisable from their large curving beak and prominent casque, they also have a distinctive dipping flight. Hornbills are monogamous and mate for life. While incubating the eggs, the female imprisons herself in a tree-trunk nest and is fed by the male.

OPPOSITE:

Chiew Lan Lake, Khao Sok National Park, Surat Thani Province
The 750-sq-kilometre (298-sq-mile) park, with the largest area of virgin rainforest in southern Thailand, is a remnant forest that has been in existence longer than the Amazon and is said to contain five per cent of the world's species. In the 1970s, Thai communists also took refuge here in the many limestone caves. Chiew Lan Lake was created by a dam in 1982 and makes for dramatic views and tourism activites.

PREVIOUS PAGES:
Beach, Ko Samui,
Surat Thani Province
A deserted beach with
coconut palms and azure
waters is for many a vision
of paradise. Until the late
20th century, coconut farming
was the main occupation on
Thailand's second largest
island. However, as by 2017
tourist numbers had reached
2.5 million and a plague
of weevils and worms had
decimated hundreds of the
coconut groves, such idyllic
views may soon be a thing of
the past.

LEFT:
Ko Nang Yuan,
Surat Thani Province
Formed by three small islands
connected to each other by
a sand bar, Ko Nang Yuan
is 15 minutes in a long-tail
boat from the larger and
somewhat infamous Ko Tao.
With no cars, the island is
more peaceful than many and
has spectacular snorkelling
opportunities. Privately
owned, no plastic bottles are
allowed and there is a small
fee to visit.

BOTH PHOTOGRAPHS:
Working Monkeys
In southern Thailand, as in many Southeast Asian countries, pig-tailed macaques have been trained for hundreds of years to pick coconuts from the high palms, with a male monkey capable of picking over 1000 per day. While concerns have been raised that the animals are being abused, others claim the monkeys live with their handlers as members of the family.

Tapi River, Surat Thani, Nakhon Si Thammarat
At 230km (142 miles), the Tapi is the longest river in southern Thailand, rising in the province of Nakhon Si Thammarat and entering the Gulf of Thailand at Surat Thani. Both river and town were renamed in 1915 after those in India to reflect their shared Buddhist heritage. Dense mangroves and nipa palms, used for thatching and weaving, line the river close to the sea.

ABOVE AND RIGHT:

Diving, Ko Samui
Diving in Ko Samui often
involves a boat trip to a more
remote island with clearer
water, but there are good sites
for both beginners and more
experienced scuba divers.
The best conditions are
between March and
September, with October
to January best avoided as
Samui, being on the gulf,
has more wind and rain
at that time.

OPPOSITE:

**Mu Ko Surin National Park,
Phang Nga Province**
Consisting of five islands in
the Andaman sea, near the
sea border with Burma, the
marine park established in
1981 has some of the best
diving in the world and the
best snorkelling in Thailand.
Key species include manta ray,
whale shark and barracuda.
The islands are inhabited by
small communities of ethnic
Moken. The park is closed
during the rainy season from
mid-May to mid-October.

ABOVE AND RIGHT:

**Oyster Farm, Ko Kaeo,
Ko Phuket**

Pearl oyster farming has been practised in Phuket for over 50 years, as the temperature of the water at between 26 and 28°C is perfect for the oysters, which are bred here and then grown in cages suspended from a bamboo structure. Saltwater pearls, of which only one can be grown per oyster, take at least five years to develop.

OPPOSITE:

**Fish Farming,
Phang Nga Bay**

Small-scale aquaculture of sea bass and grouper farming was successfully developed in Phang Nga bay in the 1980s in order to provide a livelihood for poor villagers whose fish catches had been declining every year.

Maya Bay, Ko Phi Phi, Krabi Province
Maya Bay was the unspoilt beach featured in Danny Boyle's movie *The Beach*. In order to make it appear more luscious, some existing vegetation was removed and palm trees were planted. Since then over-exploitation has led the forestry department to close the beach completely until at least 2021 in order to let the environment and, in particular, the coral recover.

OPPOSITE:

Klong Kong Beach, Ko Lanta, Krabi Province
This delightful beach has not yet been dominated by large international hotels and retains a laid-back vibe, perfect for sitting in a deckchair and sipping a cocktail or several. Ko Lanta is composed of 52 islands just off the coast of Krabi, of which the largest is Ko Lanta Yai.

LEFT:

Phuket Old Town, Ko Phuket

Phuket is one of the oldest cities in Thailand. It was where Chinese immigrants first landed from the 18th century onward and sought their fortunes in tin mining. These Hokkien Chinese married local women and created a unique community. The so-called Sino-Portuguese houses they built, are now being repurposed as attractive shops, cafes and restaurants.

RIGHT TOP:

Thai Cooking Spices and Ingredients

Thai cooking often employs many ingredients such as tamarind, kaffir lime (both the zest and the leaves can be used), lemongrass, curry powder, turmeric, roasted rice and garlic, as well as ginger, galangal and fresh chilies. Some of these are shown here.

RIGHT LOWER:

***Gaeng Leung* (Fish Curry)**

A yellow curry with either fish or prawns is a staple southern dish. The key ingredient is fresh turmeric, which imparts the colour as well as the all-important slightly sour and bitter taste. Also important is southern-style shrimp paste, which adds saltiness and richness to the dish.

OPPOSITE:
Nine Emperor Gods Festival, Phuket Town
With over half the population of Phuket identifying as Peranakan (descendants of Chinese settlers on the Malay Peninsula), the nine-day Taoist festival is energetically celebrated here. Known in Thai as the Vegetarian Festival (*Thetsakan Kin Jae*), crowds marvel at ritualized mutilations performed by in-trance devotees acting as vehicles for the descent to earth of the nine Taoist gods.

ABOVE:
Wat Khao Rang Samakhitham, Ko Phuket
The hilltop location of the Buddhist temple makes it a popular viewpoint. The large seated Buddha image with the right hand in the *vitarka*, or teaching, mudra was created by Phuket's most revered monk, Luang Pu Supha, who died in 2015, allegedly aged 118.

LEFT:

The Great Buddha, Ko Phuket

At 45 metres (148ft) high with a 25-metre (82-ft) wide base, the enormous white Buddha image in Chinese style is sited high up on Nakkerd Hills between Chalong and Kata. Built of concrete in 2004, the white jade cladding glistens in the sun and renders it visible for miles around. Funds for the project came entirely from public donation as such gifts are seen as very meritorious.

ABOVE:

Patong Beach, Ko Phuket

This almost three-kilometre (1.8-mile) long beach became popular with foreigners in the 1980s and is now the main tourist resort on the island, with a lively night-time scene. Unlike the tourists relaxing on loungers, Thai attendants – offering traditional Thai massage, drinks and tasty snacks – are completely wrapped up against the sun.

Songkhla Central Mosque, Songkhla

The largest mosque in Thailand is located between Songkhla and Hat Yai, near the large canals that form part of Hat Yai's flood defence system. The population of Thailand's three southernmost provinces are mainly Muslim, while that of Songkhla is mixed. These provinces have suffered acts of terrorism for many decades by various secessionist groups centred in Pattani, the historic Sultanate ceded to Thailand by the Anglo-Thai treaty of 1909.

LEFT:
Bird Singing Contest, Songkhla Province
Such contests are particularly popular in the South, with the most popular competition birds in Songkhla being the *nok kao chawa* (the Javanese or zebra dove). Birds are also kept in many southern homes. Winning birds are those who sing the most melodiously. Prize money can be as high as 30,000 baht (US$1000) and energetic singers can fetch hundreds of thousands of baht, with one selling for 1.5 million baht (US$30,000).

ABOVE:
Making Bird Cages, Songkhla Province
The popularity of zebra dove competitions in Songkhla has given a major boost to the local economy, whether in terms of breeding the doves, acting as dove sitters or carers and making the cages and accessories. The cages require good-quality bamboo and the more successful birds are housed in the most beautiful and expensive cages.

ALL PHOTOGRAPHS:

Thale Noi Non-Hunting Area, Phatthalung Province

The 460 sq kilometre (177 sq mile) Thale Noi is a fresh water wetland and one of the largest natural freshwater lakes in Southeast Asia, protected under the Ramsar wetlands preservation treaty.

The wetland provides a breeding habitat for tens of thousands of migratory and native birds, with 180 species recorded. The photograph to the left shows a Chinese pond heron (*Ardeola bacchus*) stepping carefully across the lily pads.

Between February and April, the shocking pink waterlilies are at their best (see right).

More than 4000 water buffalo are also farmed here, and balancing the conflicting needs of agriculture, industry and environmental protection in the face of climate change will be an ever greater challenge.

Sea Bass Cages, Songkhla Lake, Songkhla Province
Coastal aquaculture in the outer part of Songkhla lake where it adjoins the sea has been practised for almost 50 years. Seabass farming in coastal waters was pioneered in Thailand as a way of addressing declining fish stocks. Seabass, *pla krapong* in Thai, is one of the most popular fish in Thai cuisine.

LEFT:

Ko Poda, Krabi Province

The imposing karst tower stands guarding one of the bays on this uninhabited island eight kilometres (five miles) by long-tail boat from Ao Nang. The glistening white sand and clear waters full of fish are a delight, but the fear must be that the island could become the victim of its own beauty and turn into another Maya Bay.

OPPOSITE:

Pakpra, Phatthalung Province

Pakpra is a small canal that leads into Thale Noi Non-Hunting Lake. Here fisherman use traditional fishing methods of lowering bamboo square-dip nets known as *yor* in Thai and raising them when full. Recently, the area has been developed as an ecotourism destination, with visitors able to go out with the fisherman and help with the catch.

ALL:

Wat Phra Mahathat, Nakhon Si Thammarat

The main bell-shaped *chedi* of this impressive temple was
built by King Sri Dhammasokaraja in the 13th century
to enshrine a Buddha relic, allegedly one of the Buddha's
teeth. Nakhon Si Thammarat was an important town in the
Tambralinga and later Srivijaya kingdoms. The creation of
the *chedi* led to the town becoming a centre of Theravada
Buddhism and it was mentioned in Sukhothai inscriptions.

The principal *chedi* is surrounded by smaller ones and a
gallery of diverse Buddha images, some dating back to the
Sukhothai period.

The annual Hae Pha Keun That (meaning 'Processing with
a cloth up to the relic') is held to coincide with Makha Bucha
in February (see below).

ABOVE:

Nang Talung (Shadow Puppet), Phatthalung

Shadow puppetry is a traditional Thai art in which characters, cut from buffalo hide and brightly coloured, are manipulated behind a white screen for the audience out front. Unlike the larger Central Thai *nang yai*, the puppets of the southern *nang talung* have movable arms and legs. The stories shown are wide ranging, drawn from the classical *Ramakien* to popular culture and bawdy humour. About 10 puppeteers are needed, concealed in a small bamboo shelter.

RIGHT:

Buddha Statue Park, Thung Yai, Nakhon Si Thammarat Province

Hundreds of white Buddha images wait for an as-yet-to-be-built temple, referred to by Thais as 'the temple with no name'. The frequent downpours resulting from the equatorial climate of the far south create wonderful photographic opportunities at this mysterious park just off the Asian Highway.

Picture Credits